WELCOME TO THE U.S.A.
MARYLAND

Written by Ann Heinrichs   Illustrated by Matt Kania
Content Advisers: Patricia Dockman Anderson, Managing Editor,
Maryland Historical Society, and Erin Kimes, Associate Director for
Educational Programs, Maryland Historical Society, Baltimore, Maryland

The Child's World

Published in the United States of America by The Child's World®
PO Box 326 • Chanhassen, MN 55317-0326
800-599-READ • www.childsworld.com

Photo Credits

Cover: Getty Images/Taxi/Jerry Driendl; frontispiece: Photodisc.

Interior: Corbis: 6 (Paul A. Souders), 17 (Catherine Karnow), 25 (Lowell Georgia); Middelton Evans/Maryland Office of Tourism Development: 29, 34; Historic St. Mary's City: 13; Maryland Office of Tourism Development: 9 (Kent English), 14 (Dan Breitenbach), 18, 22, 26 (Leslie Kossoff), 33 (Louis Yanucci); Natalie Proctor/Piscataway Indian Museum: 10; Tim Tadder/Maryland Office of Tourism Development: 21, 30.

Acknowledgments

The Child's World®: Mary Berendes, Publishing Director

Editorial Directions, Inc.: E. Russell Primm, Editorial Director; Katie Marsico, Associate Editor; Judith Shiffer, Assistant Editor; Matt Messbarger, Editorial Assistant; Susan Hindman, Copy Editor; Melissa McDaniel, Proofreader; Kevin Cunningham, Peter Garnham, Matt Messbarger, Olivia Nellums, Chris Simms, Molly Symmonds, Katherine Trickle, Carl Stephen Wender, Fact Checkers; Tim Griffin/IndexServ, Indexer; Cian Loughlin O'Day, Photo Researcher and Editor

The Design Lab: Kathleen Petelinsek, Design; Julia Goozen, Art Production

Library of Congress Cataloging-in-Publication Data
Heinrichs, Ann.
  Maryland / by Ann Heinrichs.
    p. cm. — (Welcome to the U.S.A.)
  Includes index.
  ISBN 1-59296-445-1 (library bound : alk. paper) 1. Maryland—Juvenile literature.
I. Title.
  F181.3.H45 2006
  975.2—dc22   2005000521

Ann Heinrichs is the author of more than 100 books for children and young adults. She has also enjoyed successful careers as a children's book editor and an advertising copywriter. Ann grew up in Fort Smith, Arkansas, and lives in Chicago, Illinois.

About the Author
Ann Heinrichs

Matt Kania loves maps and, as a kid, dreamed of making them. In school he studied geography and cartography, and today he makes maps for a living. Matt's favorite thing about drawing maps is learning about the places they represent. Many of the maps he has created can be found in books, magazines, videos, Web sites, and public places.

About the Map Illustrator
Matt Kania

On the cover: Baltimore's skyline and inner harbor are breathtaking at night.
On page one: A Civil War battle took place at the Antietam Battlefield.

OUR MARYLAND TRIP

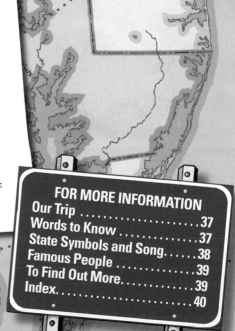

Maryland's Nicknames: The Old Line State and the Free State

4

WELCOME TO MARYLAND

Come on! Let's head out to Maryland! It's a great place to explore. Just look at all you can do.

You'll visit a space center. You'll wander through a Native American longhouse. You'll watch people making candles and churning butter. You'll meet watermen and see wild horses. You'll climb aboard sailing ships and battleships. And wait till you ride that **canal** boat. A mule pulls the boat along!

Are you ready to roll? Then buckle up, and let's hit the road!

As you travel through Maryland, watch for all the interesting facts along the way.

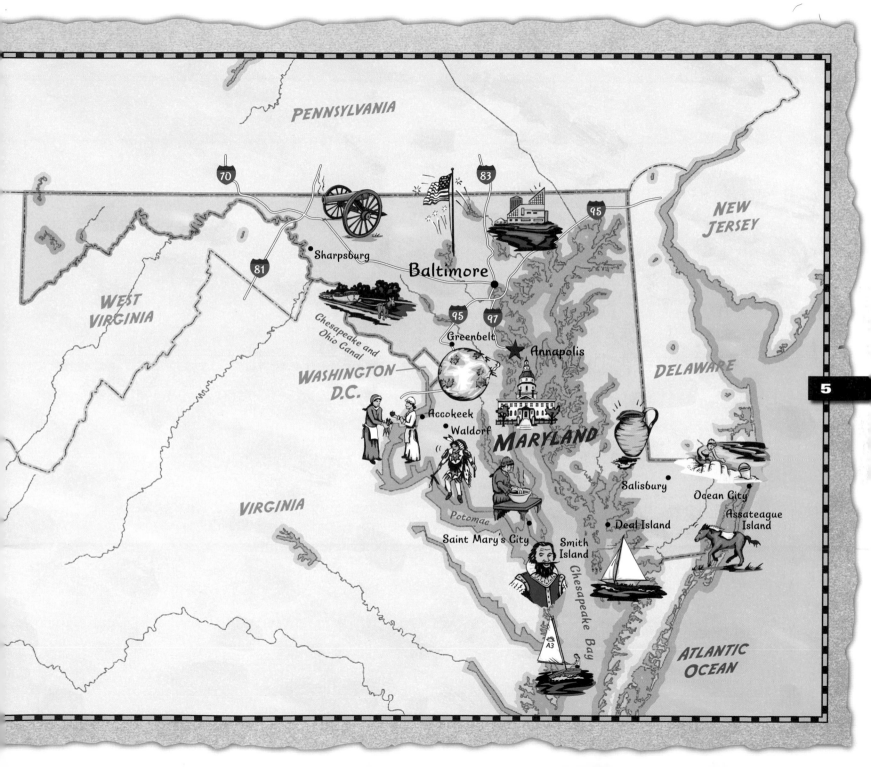

PENNSYLVANIA

NEW JERSEY

WEST VIRGINIA

Sharpsburg

Baltimore

DELAWARE

Chesapeake and Ohio Canal

95

97

Greenbelt

Annapolis

WASHINGTON D.C.

Accokeek

Waldorf

MARYLAND

Salisbury

Ocean City

VIRGINIA

Potomac

Assateague Island

Saint Mary's City

Smith Island

Deal Island

Chesapeake Bay

ATLANTIC OCEAN

Catch anything yet? This boy is fishing in Chesapeake Bay.

Take a sailboat ride or collect seashells. Discover seabirds in their nests. Go swimming or fishing. You're exploring Chesapeake Bay!

The Chesapeake Bay cuts Maryland in two. This bay is part of the Atlantic Ocean. Maryland's Western Shore is west of the bay. The Eastern Shore is east of the bay. The Eastern Shore is part of the Delmarva **Peninsula.**

Most of Maryland's rivers flow into the bay. One is the Potomac River. It forms Maryland's south and southwest borders. Western Maryland has many mountains and hills. They're part of the Appalachian Mountains.

Deep Creek is near McHenry in western Maryland. It's Maryland's largest human-made lake.

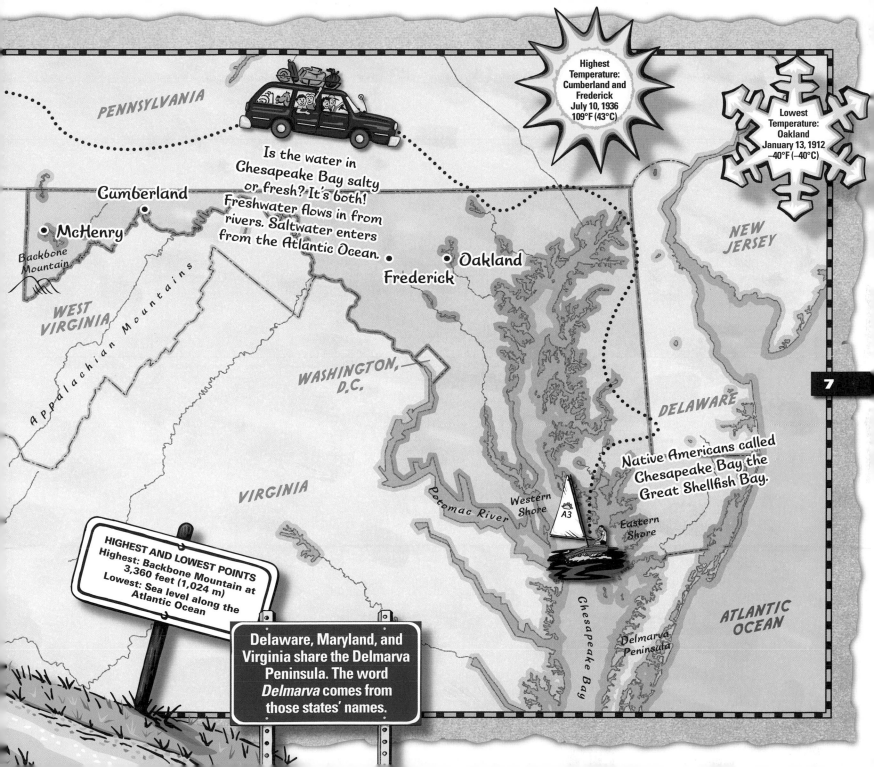

PENNSYLVANIA

Is the water in Chesapeake Bay salty or fresh? It's both! Freshwater flows in from rivers. Saltwater enters from the Atlantic Ocean.

Highest Temperature: Cumberland and Frederick July 10, 1936 109°F (43°C)

Lowest Temperature: Oakland January 13, 1912 −40°F (−40°C)

Cumberland

McHenry

Backbone Mountain

Oakland

Frederick

NEW JERSEY

WEST VIRGINIA

Appalachian Mountains

WASHINGTON, D.C.

DELAWARE

VIRGINIA

Potomac River

Western Shore

A3

Eastern Shore

Native Americans called Chesapeake Bay the Great Shellfish Bay.

HIGHEST AND LOWEST POINTS
Highest: Backbone Mountain at 3,360 feet (1,024 m)
Lowest: Sea level along the Atlantic Ocean

Delmarva Peninsula

Chesapeake Bay

ATLANTIC OCEAN

Delaware, Maryland, and Virginia share the Delmarva Peninsula. The word *Delmarva* comes from those states' names.

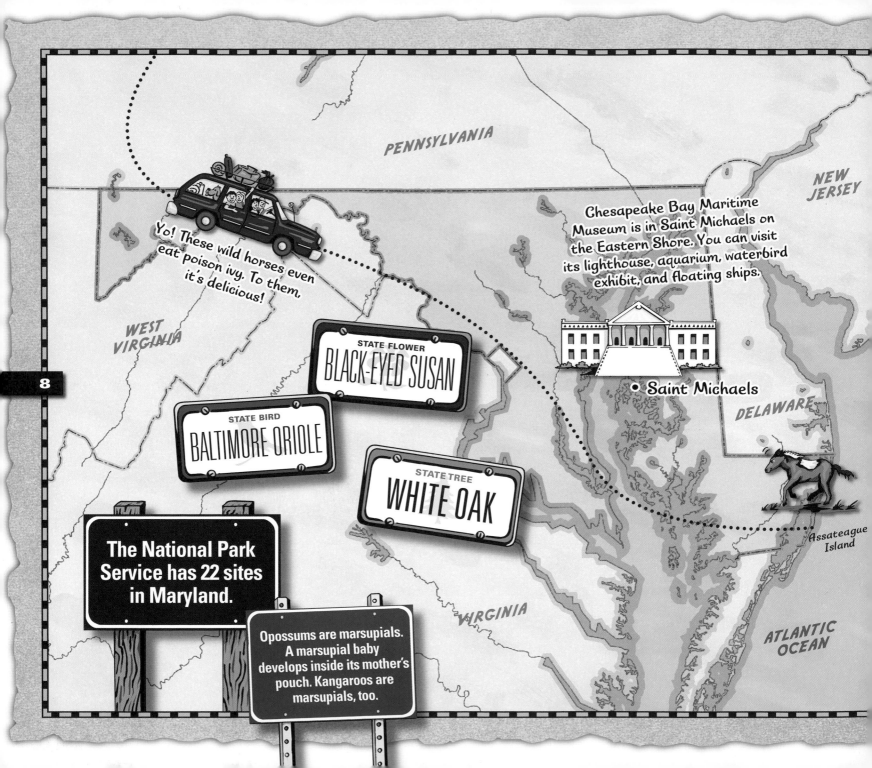

PENNSYLVANIA

NEW JERSEY

Yo! These wild horses even eat poison ivy. To them, it's delicious!

Chesapeake Bay Maritime Museum is in Saint Michaels on the Eastern Shore. You can visit its lighthouse, aquarium, waterbird exhibit, and floating ships.

WEST VIRGINIA

STATE FLOWER
BLACK-EYED SUSAN

• Saint Michaels

DELAWARE

STATE BIRD
BALTIMORE ORIOLE

STATE TREE
WHITE OAK

Assateague Island

The National Park Service has 22 sites in Maryland.

VIRGINIA

Opossums are marsupials. A marsupial baby develops inside its mother's pouch. Kangaroos are marsupials, too.

ATLANTIC OCEAN

The Wild Horses of Assateague

Roam around Assateague Island. You'll see bands of horses trotting by. But watch out. The horses are wild!

Many other animals live on Assateague. Red foxes make their homes in sand dunes. They hunt mice and birds for food. Opossums waddle around the island. They eat dead animals they find. This helps clean up the island!

Maryland's coasts are full of animal life. Seagulls, sandpipers, plovers, and egrets are some common shorebirds. Crabs, oysters, and shrimp live offshore. You'll see dolphins and whales in the water, too.

These wild horses are enjoying a day at the beach!

Assateague's wild horses are smaller than most horses. They're sometimes called ponies. A pony is a small type of horse.

There's no place like home! Furs and multicolored corncobs decorate a Piscataway longhouse.

The Piscataway Indian Museum in Waldorf

S tep inside the longhouse. It's just like its name—a long house! Deer and fox skins cover the bed. Imagine sleeping under that warm fur! Bows and arrows hang from leather cords. Multicolored corncobs are hanging up to dry.

You're visiting the Piscataway Indian Museum. There you'll see how the Piscataway people lived. They were some of Maryland's early people.

The Piscataway lived in Maryland's southern forests. They hunted with bows, arrows, and spears. They also fished and grew crops. Their trade goods reached people hundreds of miles away.

Settlers from England arrived in 1634. They founded Saint Mary's City. It was the first settlement in the Maryland **Colony.**

Cecilius Calvert sent the 1st colonists to Maryland. Calvert had the title Lord Baltimore. The city of Baltimore is named for him.

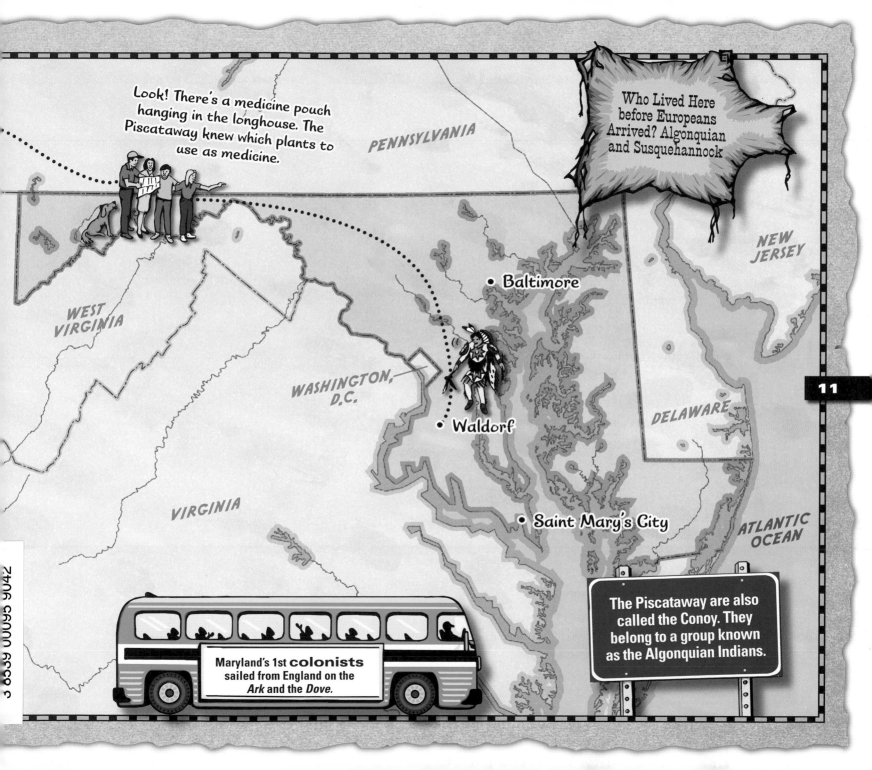

Look! There's a medicine pouch hanging in the longhouse. The Piscataway knew which plants to use as medicine.

Who Lived Here before Europeans Arrived? Algonquian and Susquehannock

PENNSYLVANIA

NEW JERSEY

• Baltimore

WEST VIRGINIA

WASHINGTON, D.C.

DELAWARE

• Waldorf

VIRGINIA

• Saint Mary's City

ATLANTIC OCEAN

Maryland's 1st **colonists** sailed from England on the *Ark* and the *Dove*.

The Piscataway are also called the Conoy. They belong to a group known as the Algonquian Indians.

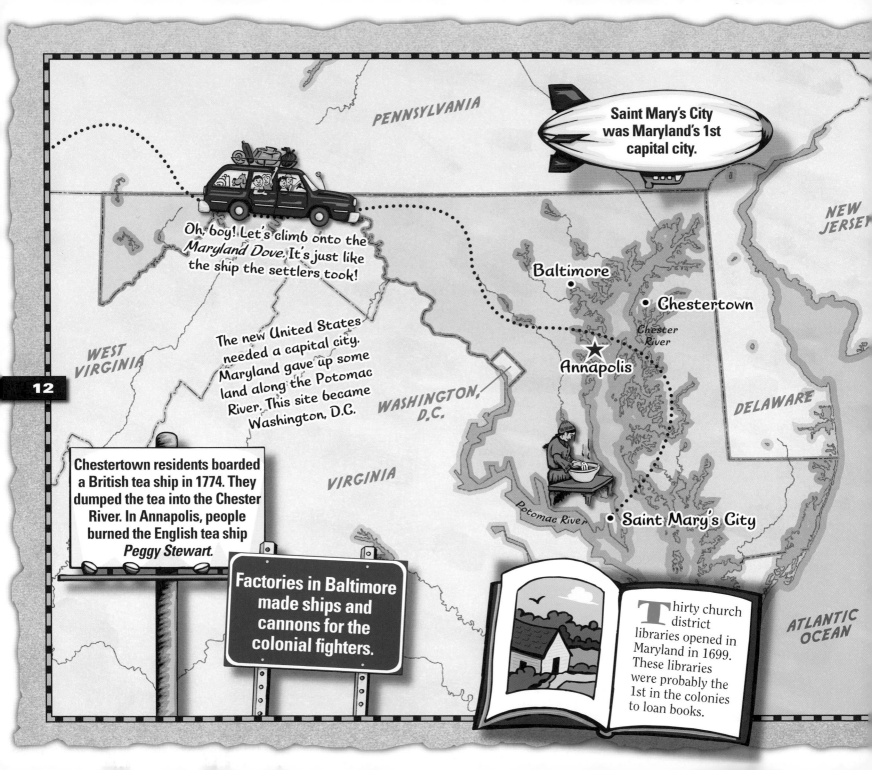

Saint Mary's City was Maryland's 1st capital city.

PENNSYLVANIA

NEW JERSEY

Oh, boy! Let's climb onto the *Maryland Dove*. It's just like the ship the settlers took!

Baltimore

Chestertown

Chester River

WEST VIRGINIA

The new United States needed a capital city. Maryland gave up some land along the Potomac River. This site became Washington, D.C.

WASHINGTON, D.C.

Annapolis

DELAWARE

12

VIRGINIA

Potomac River

Saint Mary's City

Chestertown residents boarded a British tea ship in 1774. They dumped the tea into the Chester River. In Annapolis, people burned the English tea ship *Peggy Stewart*.

Factories in Baltimore made ships and cannons for the colonial fighters.

ATLANTIC OCEAN

Thirty church district libraries opened in Maryland in 1699. These libraries were probably the 1st in the colonies to loan books.

How did Maryland's English settlers live? Just visit Historic Saint Mary's City. People in 1600s costumes show you what daily life was like. Some are working on a tobacco farm. Others work at chores such as churning butter.

Maryland was one of thirteen English colonies. The colonists hated English taxes on tea. Marylanders took action in 1774. They attacked English tea ships in Chestertown and Annapolis.

The colonists decided to fight for their freedom. They fought the Revolutionary War (1775–1783) and won! The colonies became the United States of America.

Want to see what life was like in the 1600s? Visit historic Saint Mary's City.

13

Maryland was the 7th state to enter the Union. It joined on April 28, 1788.

Lawmakers work inside the State House in Annapolis.

Name a famous general. How about George Washington? He led the colonial army in the Revolutionary War. When the war ended, he quit his job. What was his next job? First president of the United States!

Washington stood before Congress to **resign** as general. That happened in the State House in Annapolis. This building was once the nation's capitol. Now it's Maryland's capitol. State government offices are inside.

Maryland has three branches of government. One branch makes the state's laws. The governor heads another branch. It carries out the laws. Judges make up the third branch. They decide whether someone has broken a law.

The U.S. Naval Academy is in Annapolis.

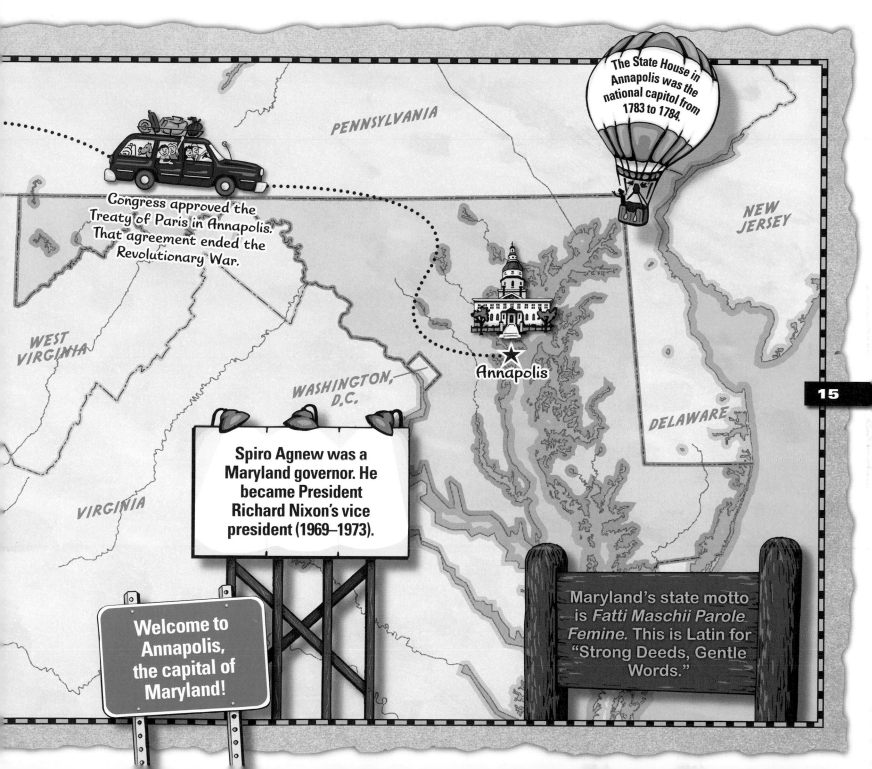

The State House in Annapolis was the national capitol from 1783 to 1784.

Congress approved the Treaty of Paris in Annapolis. That agreement ended the Revolutionary War.

PENNSYLVANIA

NEW JERSEY

WEST VIRGINIA

★ Annapolis

WASHINGTON, D.C.

DELAWARE

VIRGINIA

Spiro Agnew was a Maryland governor. He became President Richard Nixon's vice president (1969–1973).

Welcome to Annapolis, the capital of Maryland!

Maryland's state motto is *Fatti Maschii Parole Femine.* This is Latin for "Strong Deeds, Gentle Words."

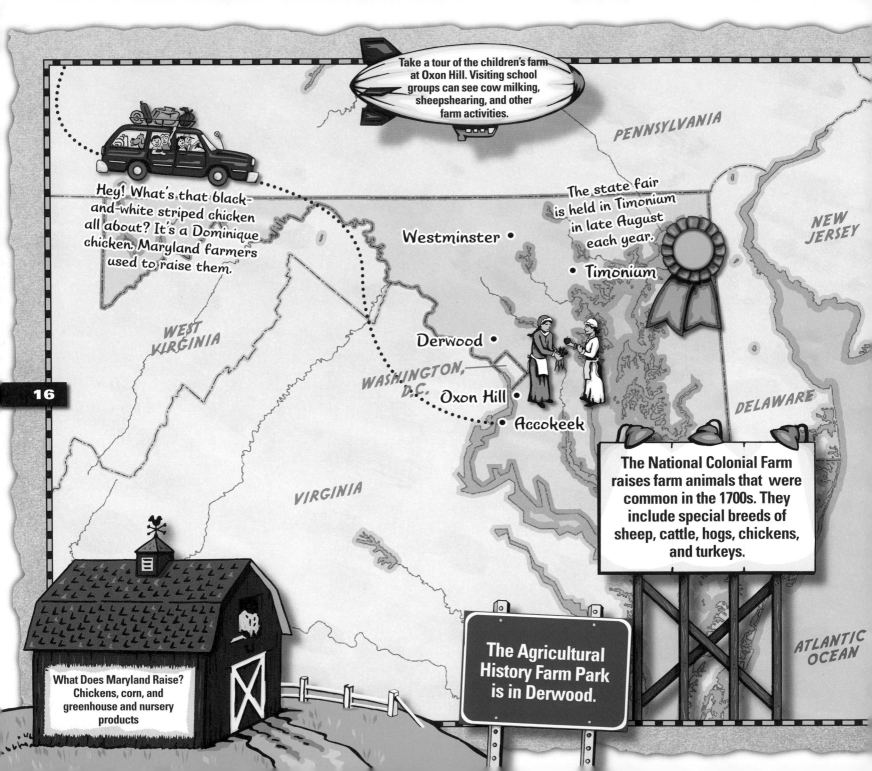

Take a tour of the children's farm at Oxon Hill. Visiting school groups can see cow milking, sheepshearing, and other farm activities.

PENNSYLVANIA

Hey! What's that black-and-white striped chicken all about? It's a Dominique chicken. Maryland farmers used to raise them.

The state fair is held in Timonium in late August each year.

NEW JERSEY

WEST VIRGINIA

Westminster •

• Timonium

Derwood •

WASHINGTON, D.C.

Oxon Hill •

• Accokeek

DELAWARE

VIRGINIA

The National Colonial Farm raises farm animals that were common in the 1700s. They include special breeds of sheep, cattle, hogs, chickens, and turkeys.

ATLANTIC OCEAN

What Does Maryland Raise? Chickens, corn, and greenhouse and nursery products

The Agricultural History Farm Park is in Derwood.

The National Colonial Farm in Accokeek

Suppose you lived on a farm in 1775. What would you do all day? Visit the National Colonial Farm, and you'll see. Its programs let you explore colonial farm life. You might feed the chickens, turkeys, and sheep. You might even grind corn or make candles.

Farming has come a long way since 1775. But chickens are still important in Maryland. Many farmers on the Eastern Shore raise chickens. Milk from dairy cows is important, too. You'll see dairy farms on the Western Shore.

Many Maryland farmers grow flowers and shrubs. Others grow corn, wheat, soybeans, or apples.

Would you have enjoyed living on a farm in the 1700s? Visit Accokeek and find out!

Carroll County Farm Museum is in Westminster. Its costumed guides give tours of many 1800s farm buildings.

Fort McHenry and "The Star-Spangled Banner"

Cover your ears! You're watching a battle reenactment at Fort McHenry.

Can you sing "The Star-Spangled Banner"? That's our national anthem. It's a song about our national flag. It tells about a fierce battle.

Do you know where that battle was? It was at Fort McHenry in Baltimore. It happened during the War of 1812 (1812–1815).

British troops attacked the fort. They fired on it all night long. Francis Scott Key watched from a few miles away. In the morning, he saw the flag waving. The British had failed to capture the fort! Key was thrilled and proud. He wrote a poem about the event. That poem became our national anthem!

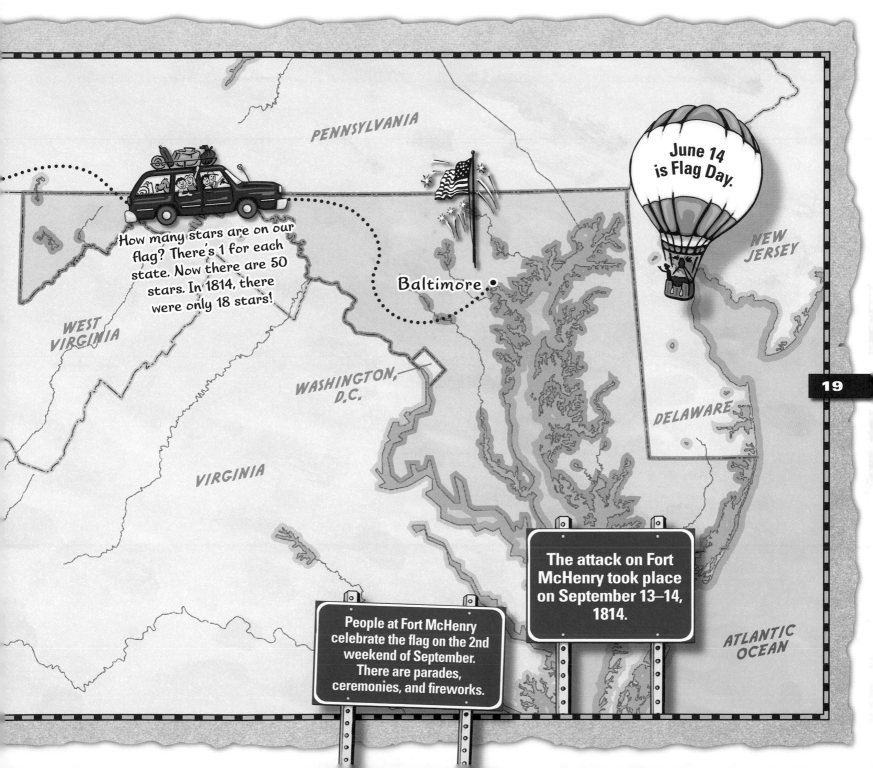

PENNSYLVANIA

June 14 is Flag Day.

NEW JERSEY

How many stars are on our flag? There's 1 for each state. Now there are 50 stars. In 1814, there were only 18 stars!

Baltimore

WEST VIRGINIA

WASHINGTON, D.C.

DELAWARE

VIRGINIA

19

The attack on Fort McHenry took place on September 13–14, 1814.

People at Fort McHenry celebrate the flag on the 2nd weekend of September. There are parades, ceremonies, and fireworks.

ATLANTIC OCEAN

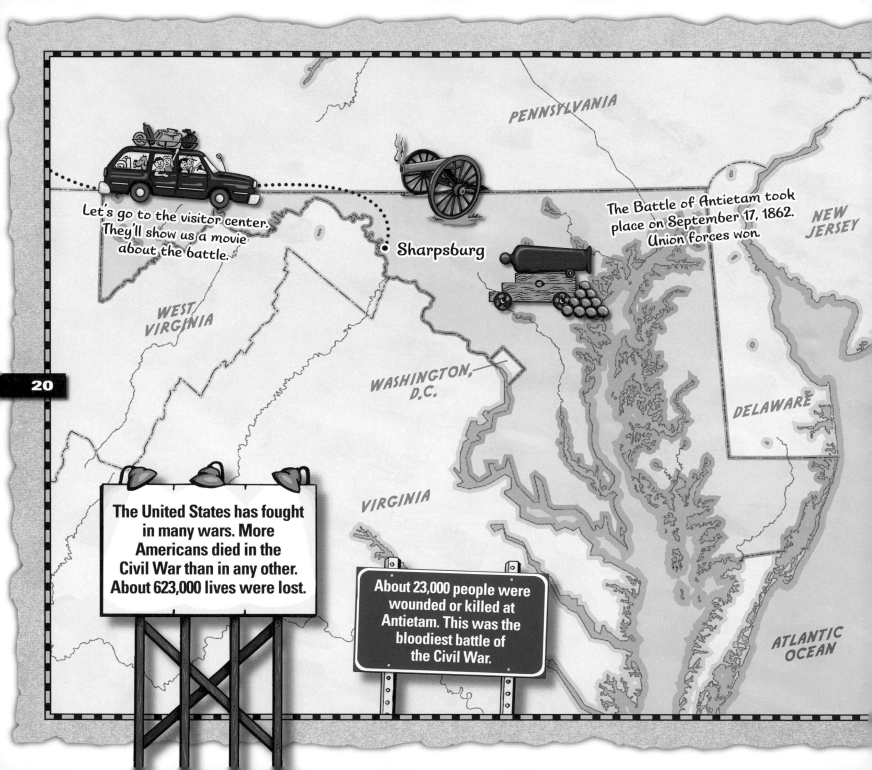

Let's go to the visitor center. They'll show us a movie about the battle.

PENNSYLVANIA

NEW JERSEY

The Battle of Antietam took place on September 17, 1862. Union forces won.

Sharpsburg

WEST VIRGINIA

WASHINGTON, D.C.

DELAWARE

VIRGINIA

ATLANTIC OCEAN

The United States has fought in many wars. More Americans died in the Civil War than in any other. About 623,000 lives were lost.

About 23,000 people were wounded or killed at Antietam. This was the bloodiest battle of the Civil War.

Walk through
Antietam Battlefield,
near Sharpsburg. Cannons point
across open fields. One pathway is
called Bloody Lane. Soldiers fought
for hours there.

This battle took place during
the Civil War (1861–1865). Northern
and Southern states fought this war.
It was about the right to own slaves.
Northern states were against slavery.
They formed the Union side. Southern
states wanted to keep slavery. They formed the Confederacy.

Some Marylanders had slaves. But Maryland stayed
in the Union. The Union won, and the slaves were freed.

Actors march at Antietam Battlefield.
They're wearing Union uniforms.

21

The Chesapeake and Ohio Canal was very important to early Marylanders.

Canal Place Heritage Area is in Cumberland. This city was at one end of the Chesapeake and Ohio Canal.

Riding Down the Chesapeake and Ohio Canal

Hop aboard the canal boat at Potomac. A mule walks along the bank. It's pulling the boat by a rope!

You're riding on the Chesapeake and Ohio Canal. People dug this waterway in the 1800s. It ran from Cumberland, Maryland, to Washington, D.C.

The canal was a big help to Marylanders. They could ship their goods on it. This was easier and cheaper than land travel. Coal from western Maryland traveled on the canal. So did lumber, grain, and other farm products. Baltimore became a big, busy city. Many ships sailed in and out of its port. Baltimore was a major shipbuilding center, too.

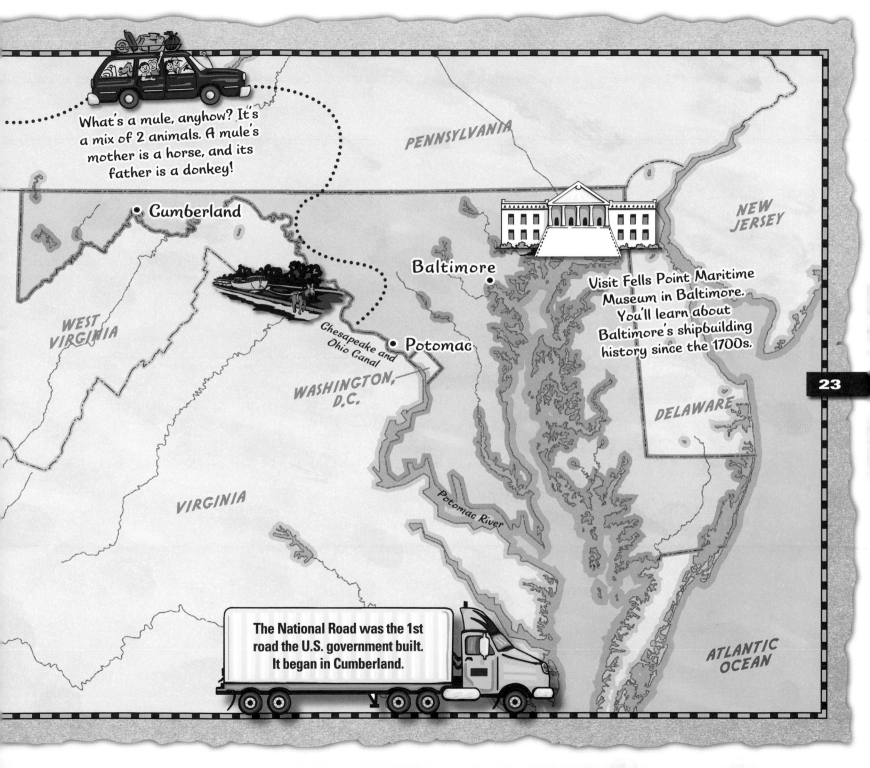

What's a mule, anyhow? It's a mix of 2 animals. A mule's mother is a horse, and its father is a donkey!

PENNSYLVANIA

NEW JERSEY

Cumberland

WEST VIRGINIA

Chesapeake and Ohio Canal

Baltimore

Visit Fells Point Maritime Museum in Baltimore. You'll learn about Baltimore's shipbuilding history since the 1700s.

Potomac

WASHINGTON, D.C.

DELAWARE

VIRGINIA

Potomac River

ATLANTIC OCEAN

The National Road was the 1st road the U.S. government built. It began in Cumberland.

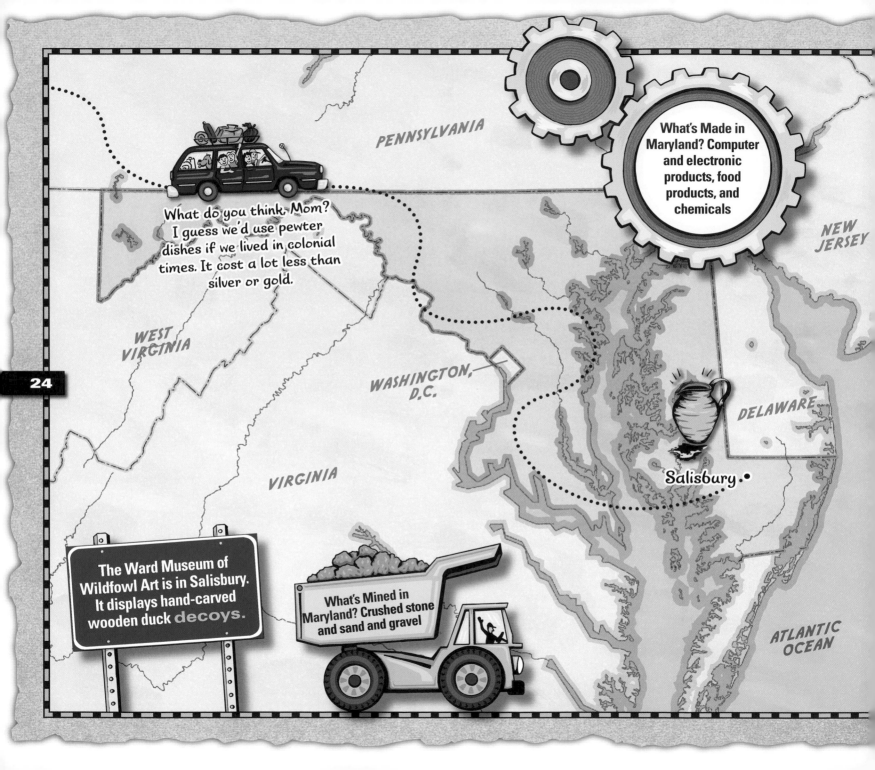

PENNSYLVANIA

What's Made in Maryland? Computer and electronic products, food products, and chemicals

NEW JERSEY

What do you think, Mom? I guess we'd use pewter dishes if we lived in colonial times. It cost a lot less than silver or gold.

WEST VIRGINIA

WASHINGTON, D.C.

DELAWARE

24

VIRGINIA

Salisbury •

The Ward Museum of Wildfowl Art is in Salisbury. It displays hand-carved wooden duck decoys.

What's Mined in Maryland? Crushed stone and sand and gravel

ATLANTIC OCEAN

The craftspeople are hard at work. They melt the metal. Then they pour it into a mold. Next, they form the metal into a shape. It might be a cup or a bowl.

You're visiting Salisbury Pewter Company. Pewter was used a lot during colonial times. It's made mostly of tin. Other metals are added to make it stronger.

Today, Maryland's factories still produce lots of metals. They make steel, aluminum, and other metals. Some shipbuilding still takes place in Maryland, too. Maryland also makes computers, airplanes, and foods.

Shipbuilding is hard work! But Marylanders are excellent craftspeople.

Goddard Space Flight Center in Greenbelt

Goddard Space Flight Center in Greenbelt

Want to see rockets and other spacecraft? Or look at pictures the space telescope took? Or learn about the latest discoveries in space? Then visit Goddard Space Flight Center!

This center is run by NASA. That's the National **Aeronautics** and Space Administration. It's one of Maryland's many U.S. government centers.

By the mid-1900s, Washington, D.C., was full of government office buildings. So the U.S. government began opening offices in Maryland. Many of them are science or medical centers. They're in towns close to Washington, D.C. This area is called Maryland's capital region.

Want to go somewhere out of this world? Visit Goddard Space Flight Center.

The Hubble Space Telescope orbits Earth. It takes pictures and gathers information about space. Scientists at Goddard send commands to the telescope.

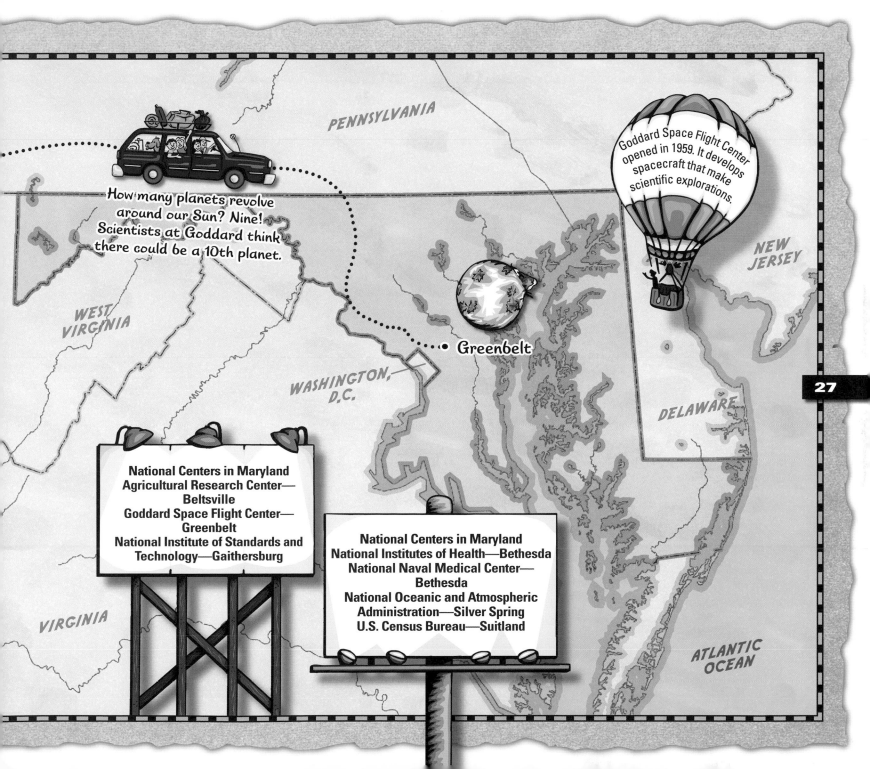

How many planets revolve around our Sun? Nine! Scientists at Goddard think there could be a 10th planet.

Goddard Space Flight Center opened in 1959. It develops spacecraft that make scientific explorations.

PENNSYLVANIA

WEST VIRGINIA

Greenbelt

WASHINGTON, D.C.

NEW JERSEY

DELAWARE

VIRGINIA

ATLANTIC OCEAN

National Centers in Maryland
Agricultural Research Center—Beltsville
Goddard Space Flight Center—Greenbelt
National Institute of Standards and Technology—Gaithersburg

National Centers in Maryland
National Institutes of Health—Bethesda
National Naval Medical Center—Bethesda
National Oceanic and Atmospheric Administration—Silver Spring
U.S. Census Bureau—Suitland

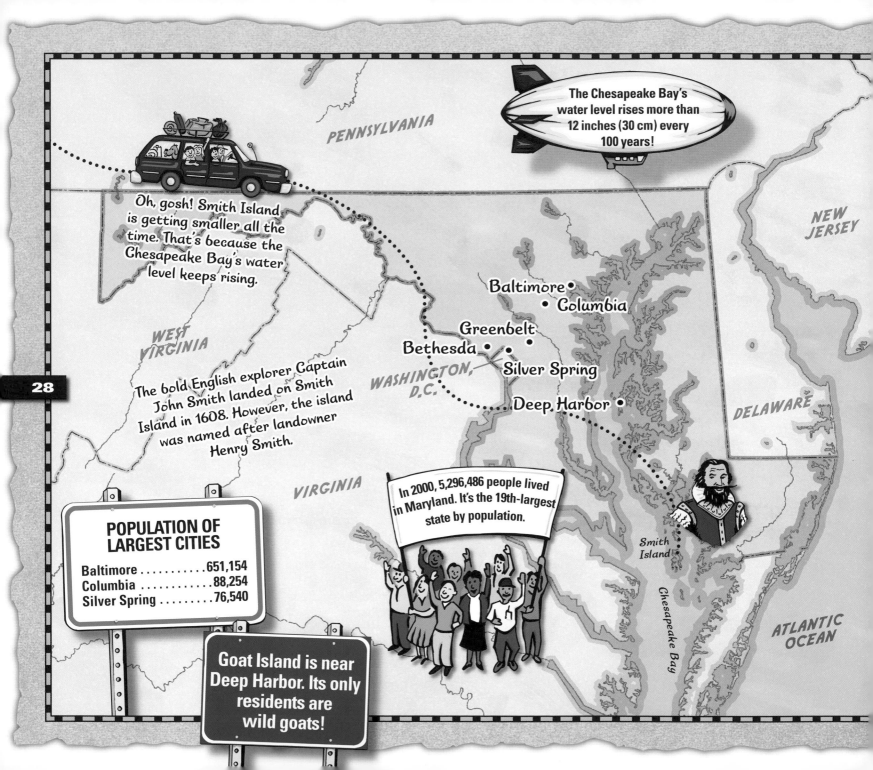

The Chesapeake Bay's water level rises more than 12 inches (30 cm) every 100 years!

Oh, gosh! Smith Island is getting smaller all the time. That's because the Chesapeake Bay's water level keeps rising.

PENNSYLVANIA

NEW JERSEY

WEST VIRGINIA

The bold English explorer Captain John Smith landed on Smith Island in 1608. However, the island was named after landowner Henry Smith.

Baltimore •
• Columbia
Greenbelt
Bethesda • •
Silver Spring
WASHINGTON, D.C.
Deep Harbor •

DELAWARE

VIRGINIA

28

In 2000, 5,296,486 people lived in Maryland. It's the 19th-largest state by population.

Smith Island

POPULATION OF LARGEST CITIES

Baltimore 651,154
Columbia 88,254
Silver Spring 76,540

Goat Island is near Deep Harbor. Its only residents are wild goats!

Chesapeake Bay

ATLANTIC OCEAN

Life on Smith Island

Visit Smith Island in the Chesapeake Bay. It's named for John Smith, the founder of Jamestown, Virginia. You'll have many surprises. There are almost no cars there. People mostly get around by walking or bike riding.

People first settled on Smith Island in 1659. They were from England and Wales. Today's residents fish for oysters and crabs. They speak an unusual form of English. It developed from the settlers' language.

People from many other lands settled in Maryland. Today, most Marylanders live in city areas. The Baltimore area has the highest population. The capital area is another big population center. Many people who work in Washington, D.C., live there.

Looking for some exercise? Visit Smith Island—you'll probably end up walking or biking.

Silver Spring, Bethesda, and Greenbelt are some cities in Maryland's capital area.

30

Skipjack Races and the Watermen

Watermen use this type of boat to fish for oysters.

Maryland's oystermen set a record in the winter of 1884–1885. They hauled in 15 million bushels of oysters!

Dozens of boats line up in the harbor. A minister blesses them for good luck. Then they're off! You're watching the Skipjack Races on Deal Island. Skipjacks are working boats. They're used for getting oysters from Chesapeake Bay.

People who run these boats are called watermen. Thousands of watermen used to work on the bay. They hauled in clams, crabs, and oysters. Their days were long and hard. They lifted heavy nets and traps. Often they were cold and wet. And there was always the danger of storms.

Not many watermen are working today. **Pollution** and other factors have reduced their catches. But watermen are still proud of their **traditions.**

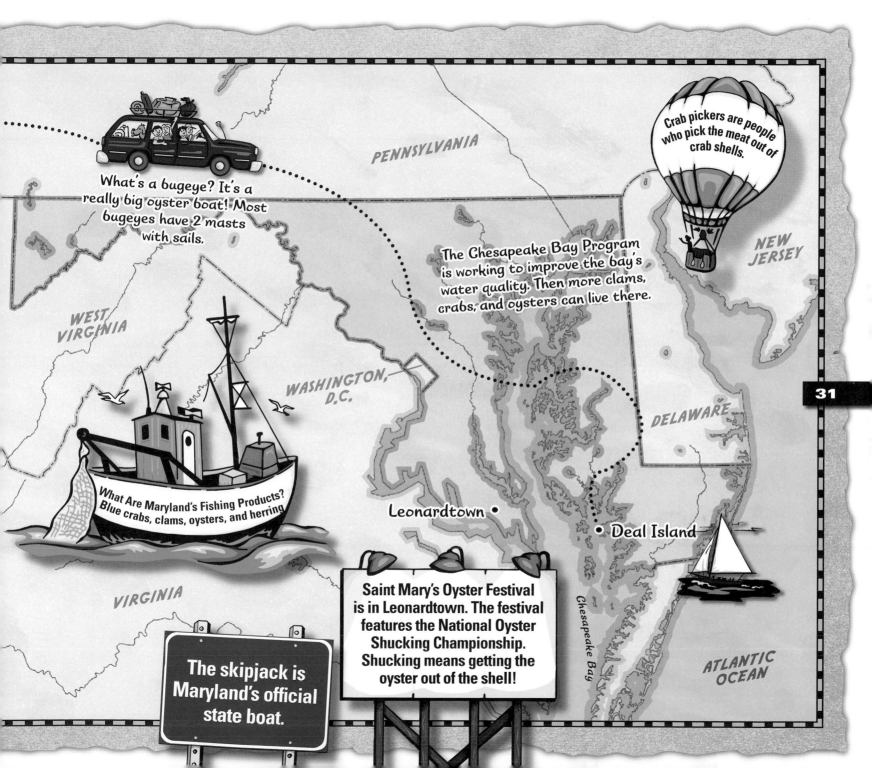

PENNSYLVANIA

Crab pickers are people who pick the meat out of crab shells.

What's a bugeye? It's a really big oyster boat! Most bugeyes have 2 masts with sails.

The Chesapeake Bay Program is working to improve the bay's water quality. Then more clams, crabs, and oysters can live there.

NEW JERSEY

WEST VIRGINIA

WASHINGTON, D.C.

DELAWARE

What Are Maryland's Fishing Products? Blue crabs, clams, oysters, and herring

Leonardtown •

• Deal Island

Chesapeake Bay

VIRGINIA

Saint Mary's Oyster Festival is in Leonardtown. The festival features the National Oyster Shucking Championship. Shucking means getting the oyster out of the shell!

The skipjack is Maryland's official state boat.

ATLANTIC OCEAN

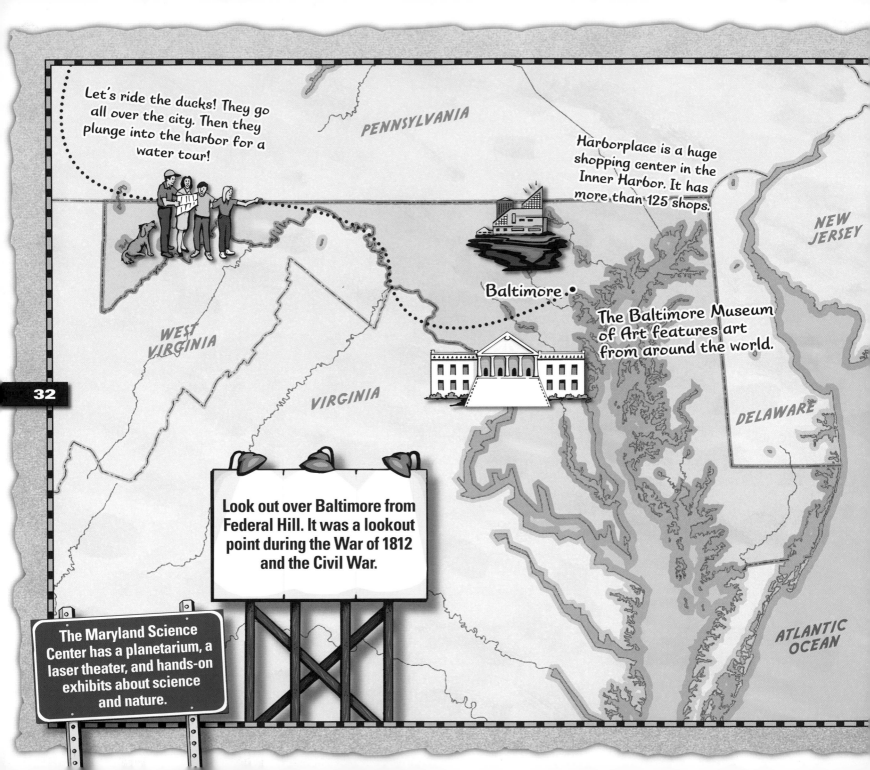

Let's ride the ducks! They go all over the city. Then they plunge into the harbor for a water tour!

PENNSYLVANIA

Harborplace is a huge shopping center in the Inner Harbor. It has more than 125 shops.

NEW JERSEY

Baltimore

The Baltimore Museum of Art features art from around the world.

WEST VIRGINIA

VIRGINIA

DELAWARE

Look out over Baltimore from Federal Hill. It was a lookout point during the War of 1812 and the Civil War.

The Maryland Science Center has a planetarium, a laser theater, and hands-on exhibits about science and nature.

ATLANTIC OCEAN

Let's Visit Baltimore!

What should you do in Baltimore? Head for the Inner Harbor! It's a popular area along the waterfront. Just walking around there is fun. You'll see street performers juggling and joking around.

It's hard to decide which museum to visit first. One is the Maryland Science Center. Or try the National Aquarium. You can see dolphin shows there.

Want to visit a place just for kids? Port Discovery is known as "The Kid-Powered Museum."

Port Discovery is fun to visit, too. It's a children's museum. Down by the dock, tour the USS *Constellation*. It was a Civil War battleship. Next, hop aboard a duck. These ducks are boats with wheels. They travel on land and water—just like ducks!

More than 2,000 animals live at the Baltimore Zoo. Many of them roam around outdoors.

Babe Ruth was a famous baseball champ. The Babe Ruth Birthplace and Museum is in Baltimore.

We're off to the races in Baltimore! Can you guess which horse will win?

Oceans of Fun in Ocean City

Zoom along on a roller coaster. Try out some video games. Then bounce around on the bumper cars. You're in Ocean City!

Ocean City is a favorite vacation spot. People play on the beach and swim. Or they stroll along the boardwalk. There's always something fun to see or do. People enjoy vacations on Chesapeake Bay, too. It's great for water sports. It's also great for watching wildlife.

Horse racing is a popular sport in Maryland. The Preakness Stakes is a famous horse race. It's held at Baltimore's Pimlico track. Jousting is another horseback sport. It used to be a battle between knights. But Marylanders do it a little more safely!

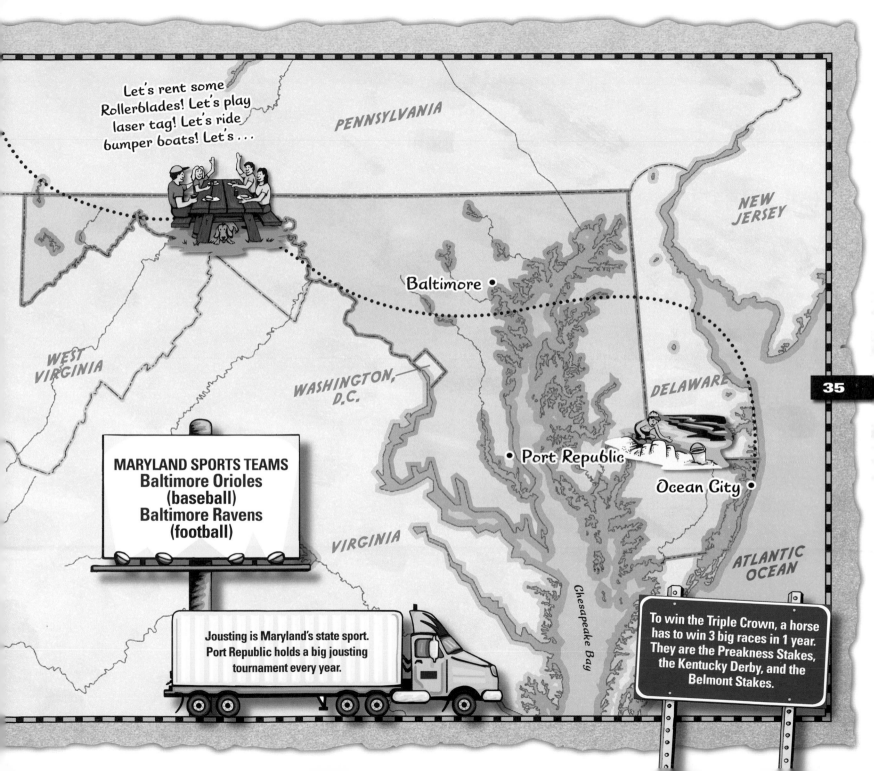

Let's rent some Rollerblades! Let's play laser tag! Let's ride bumper boats! Let's . . .

PENNSYLVANIA

NEW JERSEY

WEST VIRGINIA

Baltimore •

WASHINGTON, D.C.

DELAWARE

• Port Republic

Ocean City •

VIRGINIA

ATLANTIC OCEAN

Chesapeake Bay

MARYLAND SPORTS TEAMS
Baltimore Orioles
(baseball)
Baltimore Ravens
(football)

Jousting is Maryland's state sport. Port Republic holds a big jousting tournament every year.

To win the Triple Crown, a horse has to win 3 big races in 1 year. They are the Preakness Stakes, the Kentucky Derby, and the Belmont Stakes.

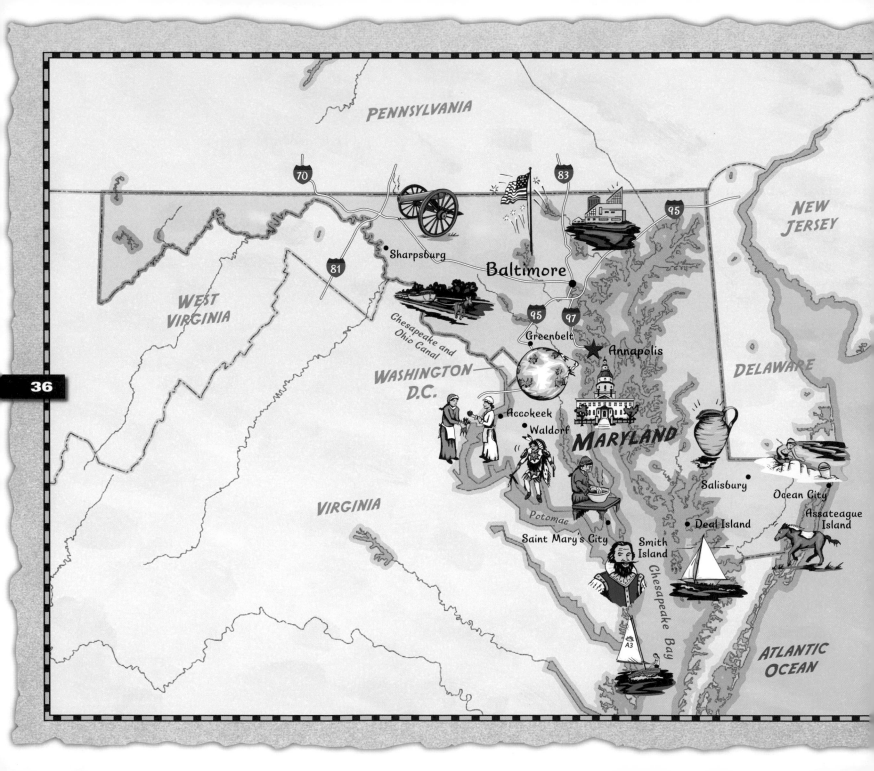

PENNSYLVANIA

NEW JERSEY

70

83

95

81

Sharpsburg

Baltimore

WEST VIRGINIA

Chesapeake and Ohio Canal

95

97

Greenbelt

DELAWARE

WASHINGTON D.C.

Annapolis

Accokeek

Waldorf

MARYLAND

Salisbury

Ocean City

VIRGINIA

Potomac

Assateague Island

Saint Mary's City

Smith Island

Deal Island

Chesapeake Bay

A3

ATLANTIC OCEAN

OUR TRIP

We visited many amazing places on our trip! We also met a lot of interesting people along the way. Look at the map on the left. Use your finger to trace all the places we have been.

What did Native Americans call Chesapeake Bay? See page 7 for the answer.

Where does a baby marsupial develop? Page 8 has the answer.

What was Maryland's 1st capital city? See page 12 for the answer.

Who was Richard Nixon's vice president? Look on page 15 for the answer.

When did the attack on Fort McHenry occur? Page 19 has the answer.

Where did the National Road begin? Turn to page 23 for the answer.

What does the Hubble Space Telescope do? Look on page 26 and find out!

How many shops make up Harborplace? Turn to page 32 for the answer.

That was a great trip! We have traveled all over Maryland! There are a few places that we didn't have time for, though. Next time, we plan to visit the Baltimore & Ohio Railroad Museum in Baltimore. Visitors learn about the history of railroads in America. They can view exhibits related to various trains and railroad equipment. If there's time left over, they can even take a train ride!

More Places to Visit in Maryland

WORDS TO KNOW

aeronautics (air-uh-NAW-tiks) the science of flying in aircraft

canal (kuh-NAL) a waterway built by humans to connect larger bodies of water

colonists (KOL-uh-nists) people who settle a new land for their home country

colony (KOL-uh-nee) a land with ties to a mother country

decoys (DEE-koiz) carved models of birds used by hunters to attract real birds

peninsula (puh-NIN-suh-luh) a piece of land almost completely surrounded by water

pollution (puh-LOO-shuhn) things such as dirt or chemicals that harm the quality of air or water

resign (ri-ZINE) to quit a job or position

traditions (truh-DISH-uhnz) customs carried on for a long time

Maryland covers 9,774 square miles (25,314 sq km). It's the 42nd-largest state in size.

STATE SYMBOLS

State bird: Baltimore oriole

State boat: Skipjack

State cat: Calico cat

State crustacean: Maryland blue crab

State dinosaur: *Astrodon johnstoni*

State dog: Chesapeake Bay retriever

State drink: Milk

State fish: Rockfish (striped bass)

State flower: Black-eyed Susan

State folk dance: Square dance

State fossil shell: *Ecphora gardnerae gardnerae* (an extinct snail)

State insect: Baltimore checkerspot butterfly

State reptile: Diamondback terrapin

State sport: Jousting

State theaters: Center Stage and Olney Theatre

State tree: White oak

State flag

State seal

STATE SONG

"Maryland's State Song"

Words by James Ryder Randall, sung to the tune of the Christmas song "O, Tannenbaum"

The despot's heel is on thy shore,
    Maryland!
His torch is at thy temple door, Maryland!
Avenge the patriotic gore
That flecked the streets of Baltimore,
And be the battle queen of yore,
Maryland! My Maryland!

Hark to an exiled son's appeal, Maryland!
My Mother State! To thee I kneel,
    Maryland!
For life or death, for woe or weal,
Thy peerless chivalry reveal,
And gird thy beauteous limbs with steel,
Maryland! My Maryland!

Thou wilt not cower in the dust, Maryland!
Thy beaming sword shall never rust,
    Maryland!
Remember Carroll's sacred trust,
Remember Howard's warlike thrust,
And all thy slumberers with the just,
Maryland! My Maryland!

Come! 'tis the red dawn of the day,
    Maryland!
Come with thy panoplied array,
    Maryland!
With Ringgold's spirit for the fray,
With Watson's blood at Monterey,
With fearless Lowe and dashing May,
Maryland! My Maryland!

Come! for thy shield is bright and strong,
    Maryland!
Come! for thy dalliance does thee wrong,
    Maryland!
Come to thine own anointed throng,
Stalking with Liberty along,
And chaunt thy dauntless slogan song,
Maryland! My Maryland!

Dear Mother! Burst the tyrant's chain,
    Maryland!
Virginia should not call in vain, Maryland!
She meets her sisters on the plain—
Sic semper! 'tis the proud refrain
That baffles minions back again,
    Maryland!
Arise in majesty again,
Maryland! My Maryland!

I see the blush upon thy cheek, Maryland!
For thou wast ever bravely meek,
    Maryland!
But lo! There surges forth a shriek,
From hill to hill, from creek to creek,
Potomac calls to Chesapeake,
Maryland! My Maryland!

Thou wilt not yield the Vandal toll,
    Maryland!
Thou wilt not crook to his control,
    Maryland!
Better the fire upon thee roll,
Better the shot, the blade, the bowl,
Than crucifixion of the soul,
Maryland! My Maryland!

I hear the distant thunder-hum, Maryland!
The Old Line's bugle, fife, and drum,
    Maryland!
She is not dead, nor deaf, nor dumb—
Huzza! She spurns the Northern scum!
She breathes! She burns! She'll come!
    She'll come!
Maryland! My Maryland!

FAMOUS PEOPLE

Banneker, Benjamin (1731–1806), mathematician and astronomer

Barton, Clara (1821–1912), founder of the American Red Cross

Blake, Eubie (1883–1983), ragtime musician and composer

Booth, John Wilkes (1838–1865), the man who killed Abraham Lincoln

Clancy, Tom (1947–), author

Douglass, Frederick (1817–1895), antislavery activist and writer

Henson, Matthew (1866–1955), explorer

Hesse, Karen (1952–), children's author

Holiday, Billie (1915–1959), singer

Hopkins, Johns (1795–1873), businessman, founder of hospital and university

Key, Francis Scott (1779–1843), lawyer and poet

Levinson, Barry (1942–), film director, screenwriter

Marshall, Thurgood (1908–1993), supreme court justice, civil rights activist

Naylor, Phyllis Reynolds (1933–), children's author

Poe, Edgar Allen (1809–1849), poet and short-story writer

Ripken, Cal, Jr. (1960–), baseball player

Ruth, George Herman "Babe" (1895–1948), baseball player

Sinclair, Upton (1878–1968), author and social reformer

Tubman, Harriet (ca. 1820–1913), antislavery activist

Waters, John (1946–), film director, screenwriter

TO FIND OUT MORE

At the Library

Bartoletti, Susan Campbell, and Claire A. Nivola (illustrator). *The Flag Maker*. Boston: Houghton Mifflin, 2004.

Burleigh, Robert, and Mike Wimmer (illustrator). *Home Run: The Story of Babe Ruth*. San Diego: Silver Whistle, 1998.

Menendez, Shirley, and Laura Stutzman (illustrator). *B Is for Blue Crab: A Maryland Alphabet*. Chelsea, Mich.: Sleeping Bear Press, 2004.

Wiener, Roberta, and James R. Arnold. *Maryland*. Chicago: Raintree, 2004.

On the Web

Visit our home page for lots of links about Maryland:
http://www.childsworld.com/links

Note to Parents, Teachers, and Librarians: We routinely verify our Web links to make sure they are safe, active sites—so encourage your readers to check them out!

Places to Visit or Contact

Maryland Historical Society
201 W. Monument Street
Baltimore, MD 21201
410/685-3750
For more information about the history of Maryland

Maryland Office of Tourism Development
217 E. Redwood Street, 9th Floor
Baltimore, MD 21202
800/634-7386
For more information about traveling in Maryland

INDEX

Bye, Old Line State.
We had a great time.
We'll come back soon!